My Repertoire

Photography CATH LOWE AT CATH LOWE PHOTOGRAPHY

Design KAREN HIBBART AT FREELANCE DESIGN & GRAPHICS

Print MARK KEY AT PIERROT

INTRODUCTION

This book is an amalgamation of my favourite dishes. You don't have to be a gifted cook to follow the recipes to create something really special. Whilst I truly hope you love my Pollyanna's Kitchen products, all of the recipes bar the Pudding section nod to them, rather than demand that you purchase each and every one. However, if you truly want the best of the best...go for it!

I have had the desire to write this book since I was a little girl. The first copy I drafted was in 2003 and I was so proud of it. I took it to a leading literary agent in London on an unheard of lunchbreak from my city job. I was to be told that whilst it was very good, I wasn't going to get a publishing deal on the basis that a) I wasn't a celeb and b) it didn't have a really unusual spin.

With my tail between my legs, I gave up.

Eighteen years later, with Pollyanna's Kitchen up and running, it felt like the time was right. Maybe I should just do it and see what happens. I feel so much of the world these days is dictated and so many people have so much to give but through fear, never do anything... and how sad is that?!

I DO believe you will love my recipes and whilst they're a rendition of our favourite classics, it doesn't matter that they aren't super fancy, or in fact, that I'm not a celeb. These are my favourites, and I am sure there are lots of things in here you will love. I must add that I am not claiming to be super healthy here, I use cream and butter and all those things Homo sapiens love, just don't eat them every day. Common-sense. Just enjoy these for what they are, and I really hope you do.

When faced with the daunting prospect of writing this book, I couldn't ever imagine having the time or patience to do it properly. Then I remembered something. If a teacher or lecturer set me a project which I had to do in a certain timeframe, I would get it done regardless of the consequences. Now I am a mum of two beautiful little boys and I put that discipline on myself. After all, it will be the most special piece I have ever done in my life.

I always ask myself, when I am an old lady, what will I look back on and regret. One thing so far that I can think of is to not write this book.

So, with no regrets, much hope and belief...I present my very first book.

My Repertoire, by me.

Pollyanna
X

MY STORY

So many people asked me how I started my business. It is a twisty-turney journey which has been full of highs and lows.

I have always had a true 'penchant' for good food. At school from a very early age, I shone in Home Economics and at every opportunity practiced my hand in the kitchen.

At the stage of 'choosing a career', going into food was something that was so exciting yet so limiting. If I was good at my game, I may have started my own restaurant, I may have been a chef or I may have gone into catering. None of which lit me up whatsoever. Being a chef in a busy kitchen with loads of shouting, being rushed and being in charge of stock control was not for me. It just wasn't glamorous enough.

I completed a four year course in International Hospitality Business Management and walked away with a first class BA degree (with honours). But what next? I knew I wanted to be in the 'big smoke', but again…doing what? A very exciting opportunity came up in Financial PR in Moorgate and I took it. During this position, I made some of the greatest friends. BUT, my heart was singing for my own business, my own path, doing something that I enjoyed.

A year earlier, my dad was diagnosed with the big C. I was knocked for six. It was already a turbulent time and my step mother was also in the advanced stages of the same disease. I found myself travelling to Tunbridge Wells to be with them almost every night on the 5.06 from London Bridge. I would arrive in the dark, make supper, then 'look forward' to catching the 5.48am back to London. It was killing me.

Three weeks before he died and on my 25th birthday, from his hospice bed, he wrote a message in a notebook. 'Good luck with Pollyanna's Kitchen, love Dad', which I only read many years later. Pollyanna's Kitchen didn't exist.

So from that point, I decided that I would live my life on his behalf. I would do everything that made me happy and spread as much love as I could. He had a real natural spark to help people and I have that spark too. Only in this instance it is presenting itself in the form of a recipe book, but going forward I truly hope I can do more to help anyone I can.

I then embarked on a professional presenting course, which landed me with the most exciting of opportunities. The face of 'Canderel'. I presented videos and voice-overs and I absolutely loved it. Sadly, it was a one-off position and once I had completed the role, that was that.

I was so desperate to do something, and an opportunity came up to take over a beautiful boutique beauty salon in Pimlico, London. At 27, I had a really exciting venture on my hands, except I was broken. I was bullied by the previous owner, so much so, sometimes I just couldn't go in. As ridiculous as it may sound, it was truly traumatic. Anyone who has been bullied will understand that feeling. It seems surreal looking back, but at the same time it' was so real to me. It was a true case of the tail wagging the dog.

I was stuck. It was as if my bank account was a free-for-all and before long, I was literally a crippled mess - unable to get out of the lease, unable to lay-off staff due to so many ridiculous factors and all whilst having a newborn baby.

It was at this point we moved to West Chiltington in West Sussex. We knew nobody there, but fell in love with the house (which needed a lot of work) and it just seemed right. I was spending two days at the house and the rest in London, going into the salon when I had the mental capacity.

Continued on next page...

Cheers!

I decided I just couldn't go on with the salon and decided to sell it. The shutters really came down from that point. I honestly think that was the hardest thing I have ever gone through. In the end, a wonderful indirect friend Angela Burnett bought the business (Moreton Place Beauty and Wellbeing) and has made a great success of it. I am eternally grateful.

I decided to throw myself into what I love and made a very clear decision to pursue it. I was going to take my favorite chilli oil recipe, perfect it, then launch it. The ol' tank was empty but I had a fierce burning desire to do it. I would put my son Julian down at 7pm, then get mixing with eight different chilli varieties (and a bottle of wine).

It was fabulous.

I put my earphones in, danced around the kitchen and threw way too many cumin seeds in each time… but eventually I decided on my perfect formula. This formula was annoyingly the same formula I had been making for years.

So, I decided to go to the Chilli Fiesta in West Dean (2016) on the scout-out for an oil company to supply my base oil and that's when I found the Cold Pressed Oil Company.

Charlie was full of advice and wisdom and without him, I honestly don't think I would ever have made a move due to fear paralysis.

I booked a stand at the Chilli Fiesta in 2017. I had 1,987 jars made up and within 21 hours of trading, I had sold out. I felt sick but high as a kite at the same time.

From that point, I just had to keep going. I didn't really know what I was doing, but I felt my way through and surrounded myself with positive, happy and supportive people. I left my comfort zone on errrr wait…too many times to count, I dreaded days where I would have to step up and show myself, but I did it. I came up against so many hurdles and people telling me I couldn't do this or that, but I have always been someone who has just bloody done it anyway. Life is too short.

Since launching Pollyanna's Kitchen, I have met so many beautiful souls and I am a much happier person for it.

So why am I writing this? Well to be fair I am a really intense cook. When I see a recipe that I like, all I can think is 'how can I put my spin on it'. There is always something I know I can do to make it better and better. I think everyone does that don't they? Add a bit more of what we like? In my case, it's always chilli and garlic, hence why I am in this game.

Thank you for buying this book. I want you to know just how much this means to me. I have struggled to get my two boys down on many a night so that I can come to my computer and type up my days work. When you're a bit of a 'this and that' cook, its actually very challenging to keep tabs!

But here I am, bones and all…doing what I want to and going it alone. It's a truly fascinating journey and I encourage anyone to do what they love. It's not about the money, it's about self-fulfillment and enjoying life doing what you love. Also setting an example to your children/people around you showing them how dreams can be achieved.

Without YOU I couldn't do this, so from the deepest part of my heart...

Thank you.

MY PRODUCTS

THE RANGE OF PRODUCTS FROM POLLYANNA'S KITCHEN

This book by no means requires that you buy all of my products, although I hope you will!

Put simply, I wanted to give a nod to my range of Artisan products and provide clear examples of how to use them every day, and in the very best ways.

All of my products contain beautiful extra virgin cold pressed rapeseed oil from the award winning 'Cold Pressed Oil Company' in Farnham. I chose this oil as it is rich in colour and has a smooth buttery taste. It is also perfect if you want to use at higher temperatures too.

My range is growing - and fast. So far, I have launched six products and received numerous Great Taste awards from The Guild of Fine Food, which makes me so happy.

So this section provides a bit of a guide and explains the similarities and differences in my products, to help you on your way to foodie nirvana.

All of my products are vegan and free from any nasties. I guarantee that every single one will provide you with freedom and versatility in your cooking, just waiting there in your fridge to save the day.

CHILLISH® - *THE ULTIMATE CHILLI OIL*

This is the original and much beloved product from Pollyanna's Kitchen and is the leading lady in the lineup of beauties in my foodie tool kit. Essentially, it is a 2-in-1 chilli oil with the best of both worlds - a ruby red, delicious chilli oil that sits on top of a rich, spicy and smoky paste – all in the same jar. The paste is what we affectionately refer to as the 'gubbins' and if you read on further you will see this cheeky 'gubbins' has taken a step up and made it as a product in its own right, it is that good!

Made using a secret blend of ingredients, Chillish® contains caramelised shallots, garlic and spices. The oil and the gubbins can be used separately, for instance the oil part can be sploshed generously in a frying pan to give onions and vegetables a head start in the flavour stakes and then the gubbins at the bottom can be used to add as a paste to the finished dish or as a garnish. Or some people like to shake the jar up to combine it all together and use it that way. They are way ahead of the game.

Continued on next page...

CHILLISH® SUPER HOT – *THE ULTIMATE CHILLI OIL* (Hot)

Stand back guys! We are coming in hot! This one is brand new and ready to rock your world. Super Hot is the latest creation in Pollyanna's Kitchen and it comes with a friendly warning as per the label - yes it's SUPER HOT.

Heat, power and flavour. Watch out for that paste. It's the chilli fanatic's favourite, and one that they just can't get enough of, but are also slightly scared of at the same time. Try it at your own risk, just don't come crying to me afterwards. This is chilli oil + paste for brave humans who like it H.O.T.

CHILLISH® MELLOW – *THE ULTIMATE CHILLI OIL* (Mild)

If you can't stand the heat then....try this! With all the delicious flavour of our original Chillish® but without any of the heat, this is a winner if you are cooking for children or adults who just don't like things spicy. It's the same concept as Chillish® i.e. oil and paste together in the same jar, but with Chillish® Mellow you have a pleasingly cool chilli oil and gubbins, to use as you wish, safe in the knowledge that all of the flavour will be there but you won't get a tingle on your tongue. Say hello to Mellow and you will win over the hearts and taste buds of your nearest and dearest. A great time to start them slow and steady on their chilli journey, with a gentle hand-holding on the way...maybe don't mention Super Hot just yet...'baby steps'.

GARLISH® – *THE ULTIMATE GARLIC OIL*

This is, without a doubt, your best friend in the kitchen. Its uses are so numerous I could fill this whole book with a huge list of what it can do, way beyond making the most insane garlic bread or garlic new/roasted potatoes (which I could eat forever and ever).

The jar of Garlish® itself is mostly filled with a dreamy, golden-yellow garlic oil, with the most wonderfully fragrant rich garlic paste in it too. No more peeling, chopping and cooking or roasting garlic. Garlish® is there at a moment's notice to slather itself over meat, fish or veggies before cooking, to liven up and add garlicky depth to any dish, gravy, dip, dressing, sauce, the list is endless. Well rounded and just the most perfect garlic taste.

Continued on next page...

GARLISH® JUST THE CRUSH –
INTENSE GARLIC PASTE

To me, the smell of Garlish® Just The Crush is like summer in a jar. It is that tantalising moment when you're on holiday somewhere warm and sunny and you get a heady waft of garlic from a nearby restaurant as you walk by. Impossible to ignore and it makes you feel very happy inside. Garlish® Just the Crush will evoke those feelings of summer, even in the coldest depths of winter when the rain is pouring down outside and you're dreaming of being in sunnier climes. The paste is predominantly cooked garlic, with added shallots and herbs to add even more depth of flavour. I urge you to add it to dishes you cook on a regular basis and experiment with a few new dishes to see what you like. The garlic is so well balanced that frying with it or using on a BBQ is not advised – use Garlish® oil instead. Garlish® Just The Crush is best used as a brilliant garlic seasoning or condiment, when whatever you are cooking or making is removed from the heat or to stir into something delicious for that perfect roasted garlic aroma, without any fuss or faff.

CHILLISH® JUST THE GUBBINS –
INTENSE CHILLI PASTE

The 'gubbins' in Chillish® Chilli Oil was so popular, that we had to make it a stand-alone product to please our raving fans and chilli-obsessed followers.

It is an intense, ready-to-eat chilli paste, but without the amount of oil you will find in Chillish®. It is more of a gooey, fragrant and versatile condiment or relish, which can also be used as a marinade, condiment, stir-in or mixer. It works well placed on the table when you're eating as an accompaniment for a quick chilli kick, to pep up any dish (or person) that needs a little oomph.

A LITTLE CHAT ABOUT...

There are a few important things to remember when cooking. I have a wee bee in my bonnet about the following:

CHICKEN

Oh Lordy, chicken is such a minefield. Please, all I ask is that you buy good quality chicken, from a reputable source. Cheap-o chicken will be sad, tough and quite frankly...rank. You'll taste the difference. Cheaper chicken will look all nice and plump but cook it and you'll see the meat shrink as the water comes out of the flesh (where they have injected it to make it look plump!) and it will ruin everything. Not only the taste, but the whole cooking process. Please trust me. Buy good quality chicken and you'll see the difference. Don't jeopardize your dish!

Bone-in chicken thighs with skin will always win over a dry and manky ol' breast.
The thigh meat has a much richer flavour, so please where you can, use thighs not breasts!

BEEF & LAMB

Again, please make sure you buy good quality. If you buy cheap meat it can ruin a dish through drowning everything – especially onions, which are trying to dry out and caramelise!

ONIONS

Now here's the thing. Onions are absolutely essential in a huge amount of dishes, but you need to cook them properly. If you undercook them, they don't really offer anything and if you burn them, you need to chuck them. The best scenario is to 'caramelise' them. This is where they are cooked over a moderate heat and the sugars start to change and they turn sweet and caramelly. It's actually a chemical process! They really are magic – just be patient with the cooking process.

SPICES

Fresh is always best! Have a pestle & mortar on hand because this will smash them up and release the beautiful fresh flavours. Choose the right one and they look pretty snazzy on your kitchen surface.

MEAT AND SEAFOOD 'RESTING'

100% both of these chaps need a rest after cooking. Please make sure you do this. If you don't, you risk loads of juice, which is great for gravy but not good for the meat. I remember watching a program that Heston did. He fried two steaks in exactly the same way. He took them both off the heat and placed a large Perspex sheet over one steak and stood on it… which produced an instant steak – juice Tsunami. The other steak he left for 20 minutes and then stood on it. Hardly anything escaped as it had been absorbed. Clever-sausage-Heston hereby demonstrated that resting is SO IMPORTANT. Although fish has much shorter connective tissue, you should still rest it for 10 or so minutes to let the tight bonds in the flesh relax. You'll see the difference.

*"Everything in moderation,
including moderation itself."*

Oscar Wilde
Irish poet and fellow foodie

CONTENTS

"Feel the fear and do it anyway."

Susan Jeffers

STARTERS/LIGHT BITES

CHILLISH® MACKEREL PÂTÉ & CORNICHONS
with Toasted Sourdough

A beautiful pâté which goes that extra mile. Mackerel is full of flavour and the Chillish® sets it off on the right foot. All in all, this is an absolute winner.

Serves: 4 people

INGREDIENTS:

4 fillets of smoked mackerel

2 tsp horseradish

2 tsp Dijon mustard

2 tbsp Chillish® Just the Gubbins

A handful of dill (finely chopped)

3 tbsp crème fraîche

Salt and pepper

Juice of ½ a lemon

50g butter (soft)

2 tsp paprika

A handful of cornichons (sliced)

150g melted butter (for topping)

A handful of chives (finely chopped)

4 slices of toasted sourdough

METHOD:

1. Remove the skin from the fish and add to a large bowl. Sift through the meat and discard any tough bits and bones.

2. Leaving aside the soft butter and cornichons, add the remaining ingredients to the mackerel and vigorously mix together until it forms a paste-like consistency.

3. Add the cornichons and soft butter and mix well.

4. Spoon the mixture into individual ramekins and pat down until smooth. Set aside.

5. To make the topping, melt the butter in a pan or microwave, then pour it over each pâté.

6. Once cooled, place in the fridge for 2 hours until the butter has hardened.

7. Before serving, sprinkle with chives and serve with toasted sourdough.

Chef Pollyanna's KITCHEN

CRISPY BREADED CAMEMBERT
with a Chillish® & Honey Infusion

If you always order this when you see it in a restaurant, you NEED to give it a go. I use a disposable glove whilst breading the cheese as it can get a bit messy. It is so incredibly straightforward to make and you will not believe how delicious it is. The Chillish® just sets it off beautifully. It is very rich, so one triangle each before a main meal, I find works well. Please make sure the Camembert is very cold before using it otherwise it will leak. I always keep one in the fridge for emergencies.

Serves: 4 people

INGREDIENTS:

1 whole Camembert (divided into 4 triangles)

5 tbsp Garlish® oil

4 handfuls mixed salad leaves

1 egg

3 (heaped) tbsp plain flour

1 tbsp paprika

1 tbsp mustard powder

2 tsp dried parsley

1 tsp salt

A few grinds of ground black pepper

Breadcrumb Mix:

5 (heaped) tbsp course breadcrumbs

Infusion:

2 tbsp Chillish® Just the Gubbins

5 tbsp honey

METHOD:

1. Mix the **Infusion** together and set aside.

2. Put the flour in a bowl.

3. Put the breadcrumb mix on another plate and mix well.

4. Whisk the egg in another bowl.

5. One by one, coat each triangle in the flour, then the egg and then the **breadcrumb mix**. Make sure that each side is fully coated.

6. Heat the Garlish® oil in a frying pan. When piping hot, add the breaded triangles. Fry on all sides, turning regularly, until they are browned.

7. Place a handful of mixed leaves on each plate, followed by the Camembert. Drizzle over the **infusion** and serve immediately.

23

CHILLISH® PRAWN COCKTAIL
with Avocado

An old classic with a punchy twist. Some people have used Tabasco in the cocktail sauce, but I think Chillish® Just the Gubbins gives it that flair and depth of flavour it needs.

Serves: 4 people

INGREDIENTS:

300g cooked king prawns

2 just ripe avocados

Juice of ½ lemon

2 sweet gem lettuces (chopped)

Cocktail Sauce:

A handful of dill (finely chopped)

3 tbsp mayonnaise

1 tbsp Chillish® Just the Gubbins

2 tbsp tomato ketchup

3 tbsp Worcestershire sauce

1 tbsp horseradish

2 tbsp tomato purée

Juice of ½ a lemon

Salt and pepper

Garnish:

Chives (chopped)

4 lemon wedges

METHOD:

1. To make the **cocktail sauce**, mix all of the ingredients together in a bowl and generously season with salt and pepper. Stir in the peeled prawns.

2. Peel the avocados and cut into cubes. Lightly toss in the lemon juice.

3. Divide the lettuce between 4 glasses and arrange the avocado on top. Spoon the prawn mixture over the avocado and garnish with a lemon wedge and a sprinkling of chives.

Serve with buttered brown bread.

GARLISH® & LEMON PRAWN POTS
with Crusty Bread

A rich and decadent starter that always goes down a storm. You can easily serve this as a 'one pot' casual dipping dish for a quick lunch. I always have a big bag of raw king prawns in the freezer, which not only is more cost-effective but it means I can whip up a stunner at the drop of a hat.

Serves: 4 people

INGREDIENTS:

300g raw king prawns

1 small onion (finely diced)

A good slosh of Garlish® or Chillish® oil

3 (heaped) tbsp Garlish® Just the Crush

1 tsp paprika

150g single cream

50g butter

Juice from 1 lemon

1 tsp plain flour

A good slosh of dry white wine

A handful of fresh parsley (save a few leaves for garnish)

1 ripe tomato (finely chopped)

1 tsp salt

A few good crunches of black pepper

A handful of Parmesan (grated)

Fresh crusty bread

METHOD:

1. Preheat the grill to 200°C.

2. On a medium heat, fry the onion in the oil and butter for 10 minutes until soft and caramelised.

3. Add the tomato and continue to fry for 5 minutes.

4. Add the flour and paprika, stir well, then add the wine. Increase the heat and when the wine has reduced a little, lower the heat and add the prawns and lemon juice. Cook for a further 3-4 minutes until the prawns are cooked.

5. Stir in the Garlish® Just the Crush, cream and parsley. Add the salt and pepper.

6. Stir well, then evenly decant into individual ramekins, or one sharing dish. Sprinkle with Parmesan and place under the grill for 2 minutes. Garnish with the remaining parsley.

Serve with crusty bread.

SEARED SCALLOPS & CRISPY PANCETTA
with a Minted Garlish® Pea Crush

Now this has to be one of the easiest recipes going. The flavours, textures and presentation, puts this up there with the stars! Scallops are relatively easy to get hold of and you can always keep a supply in the freezer, just make sure they are cooked all the way through.

Serves: 4 people

INGREDIENTS:

16 raw scallops (4 each)

60g diced pancetta

2 cups of petit pois peas (defrosted)

A large handful of fresh mint leaves

1 tsp salt

1 tsp sugar

3 tbsp Garlish® Just the Crush

A good slosh of Garlish® oil

A large knob of butter

A few grinds of black pepper

METHOD:

1.   In a frying pan, on a high heat, add the Garlish® oil and fry the Pancetta until it is crispy. Remove with a slotted spoon (leaving the oil) and set aside.

2.   Blend the peas, mint, Garlish® Just the Crush, salt and sugar. Add to a second pan and bring to a gentle simmer.

3.   Reheat the leftover oil and add the butter. Turn up the heat and then add the scallops. Fry for about 3 minutes, turning every 10 seconds until the scallops are cooked through and nicely browned.

4.   Add the Pancetta, then remove from the heat.

5.   Spread the pea purée on each plate, then place the scallops and pancetta on the top.

Serve immediately.

CHICKEN

31

ROAST CHICKEN PIE
with Truffle & Puff Pastry

I have always loved chicken pie. It is one of those dishes that is so incredibly comforting. This recipe is famous in my household and I am always asked to make it when we have guests. It is dreamy on every level. You can of course use left-over roast chicken if you have enough, but please be sure to add some leftover gravy too! Also, if you're feeling fancy, you can 'lattice' the pastry by cutting it into strips and intertwining it. I love homemade pastry but, in all honesty, pre-rolled puff is so good these days and will save you so much time.

Serves: 4 people

INGREDIENTS:

1 whole chicken
A good slosh of Garlish® oil
1 leek (sliced)
1 onion (diced)
30g butter
1 tbsp plain flour
100ml double cream
A large handful of petit pois peas (frozen)
2 tbsp Garlish® Just the Crush

2 tbsp truffle oil
2 tbsp thyme leaves
100ml sherry
2 chicken stock cubes (crumbled)
Salt and black pepper

Topping:
320g (1 packet) puff pastry (sheet)
1 egg

METHOD:
1. Preheat the oven to 170°C.
2. Place the whole bird on a baking tray and drizzle with some Garlish® oil, then season with salt and black pepper. Place in the oven and cook for 1hr and 20 minutes.
3. In a pan, add the butter and another slosh of oil. Add the onion and leek and fry on a medium heat until they are translucent and slightly browned.
4. Add the flour and stock cubes. Stir well.
5. Slowly pour in the sherry and increase the temperature whilst stirring continuously, for 1 minute. Turn the heat down low and add the thyme, peas and Garlish® Just the Crush.
6. Once the chicken is cooked (please make sure the juices are running clear), set aside for 10 minutes to rest. Add any leftover juices from the chicken and discard any fat where you can. Bring to a simmer and allow the sauce to thicken slightly. Turn the oven up to 200°C.
7. Remove pieces of chicken from the bone and place them in a rectangular ovenproof dish. Don't forget to get the oysters underneath! They are the best bit.
8. Add the cream and truffle to the sauce and stir well. Then, pour over the chicken pieces and lightly mix together.
9. Unroll the pastry and simply lay it over the top of the dish. Lightly score the edges with a sharp knife, then brush the top with a beaten egg.
10. Place in the oven for approximately 20 minutes until the pastry is golden and has risen.

GARLISH® STUFFED CHICKEN BREAST

with Proscuitto & Asparagus

I generally find chicken breasts pretty boring, however by stuffing them with Garlish® first, it gives them an almighty upgrade! This is a very easy meal all around and it really looks like you have gone to a lot of trouble.

Serves: 4 people

INGREDIENTS:

4 free-range chicken breasts

A good slosh of Garlish® oil

8 slices of Proscuitto

8 sundried tomatoes (roughly chopped)

16 asparagus spears (trimmed)

8 tsp Garlish® Just the Crush

A handful of Parmesan shavings

Salt and black pepper

METHOD:

1. Preheat the oven to 170°C.

2. Slice each chicken breast down one side, to create a pocket. Add two teaspoons of the Garlish® Just the Crush, two chopped sundried tomatoes, followed by four asparagus tips.

3. Close the breast and wrap each one in two slices of Prosciutto.

4. In a large pan, bring a generous slosh of Garlish® oil to a high temperature and add each chicken breast, regularly turning so they don't burn.

5. Once the Prosciutto has nicely browned, place the breasts into an oven dish and pour over any juices from the pan. Sprinkle with salt and pepper and place (uncovered) in the oven for 15 minutes, until the chicken has cooked through.

6. Once cooked, remove from the oven, sprinkle with Parmesan, then cover in foil. Set aside and leave to rest for 5 minutes.

7. Once ready, place each breast on a plate. Divide the remaining juices between the four plates, then sprinkle with the Parmesan shavings.

Serve immediately.

35

GARLISH® TARRAGON CHICKEN
with Sherry & Crème Fraîche

This is my spin on the classic French dish 'Poulet à l'Estragon', which brings together some of the most beautiful ingredients on earth, to make something rather outstanding. This is a dish that I do time and time again. Leaving the skin on the chicken is essential, as is buying fresh tarragon. You just can't beat it. Serve with fluffy basmati rice.

Serves: 4 people

INGREDIENTS:

8 chicken thighs (skin on & on the bone)

A good slosh of Garlish® oil

20 small round shallots (peeled and halved)

3 tbsp Garlish® Just the Crush

150ml crème fraîche

2 handfuls of tarragon leaves

100ml sherry vinegar

500ml sherry

1 chicken stock cube (crumbled)

1 tbsp flour

2 tbsp Dijon mustard

Salt and black pepper

METHOD:

1. Add a good slosh of Garlish® oil to a heavy-based pan and turn up to a high heat.

2. Generously season the chicken thighs with salt and pepper, then fry them until they are browned all over – especially the skin. Remove and set aside.

3. In the same pan, add the halved shallots. When they are nicely browned, add the chicken (including juices) back to the pan and sprinkle with the flour. Mix well.

4. Next, add the sherry, the sherry vinegar, the chicken stock and one handful of tarragon leaves. Bring to the boil, stirring continuously for 1 minute.

5. Turn the heat down to a gentle simmer, then stir in the Garlish® Just the Crush and mustard. Put the lid on and cook for 45 minutes, or until the chicken is cooked and tender.

6. Add the crème fraîche and simmer for a further 10 minutes, uncovered. Season to taste then sprinkle with the remaining handful of tarragon leaves.

CHICKEN BASQUE
with Olives & Sundried Tomatoes

This dish originates from 'the Basque country' which straddles the border between Spain and France. I have no idea how paprika made it into the mix, but either way, it works…and it works beautifully. I remember my mother cooking this when I was a little girl. I had never tasted anything so delicious. Paprika has to be up there as one of my favorite spices and as you'll see, I don't hold back. You can use any type of paprika for this dish.

Serves: 4 people

INGREDIENTS:

8 chicken thighs (skin on and on the bone)

A good slosh of Chillish® or Garlish® oil

3 tbsp Garlish® Just the Crush

2 tbsp Chillish® Just the Gubbins

4 tbsp of paprika

2 handfuls of basil leaves (chopped)

500g brown basmati rice

200g sundried tomatoes

2 red peppers (sliced into strips)

1 red chilli pepper (sliced)

600ml white wine

100ml chicken stock

4 tbsp tomato purée

Salt and black pepper

METHOD:

1.   Preheat the oven to 160°C.

2.   In a large ovenproof saucepan, add the Garlish® oil and turn up to a high heat.

3.   Generously season the chicken thighs and add to the pan. Once nicely browned on all sides, sprinkle with 2 tbsp of paprika. Remove the thighs with a slotted spoon and set aside.

4.   Lower the heat to medium and add another slosh of Garlish® oil. Add the rice, peppers and remaining paprika. Fry for 5 minutes.

5.   Next, stir in the Chillish® Just the Gubbins, tomato purée, sundried tomatoes, half of the basil and Garlish® Just the Crush.

6.   Add the white wine and stock liquid. Increase the heat and continually stir for 2 minutes. Season with plenty of black pepper and salt, then turn off the heat.

7.   Carefully sink each of the chicken thighs (skin up) on top of the rice. Drizzle over any remaining juices.

8.   Place in the oven and cook (covered) for 1 hour 20 minutes.

9.   When ready, sprinkle with any remaining basil leaves and the chopped chilli pepper. Serve in the original pan and encourage people to simply serve themselves.

PULLED CHILLISH® CHICKEN THIGH WRAP

with Avocado & Red Onion

I always use chicken thighs – simply put, they have a much softer texture AND have better flavour than breast meat. This recipe makes a superb lunch and an even better use of left over roast chicken. You can use a tortilla wrap, brioche bun, pitta, in fact anything you have. Consider this a magical filling for anything… even over a jacket potato.

Serves: 2 people

INGREDIENTS:

4 chicken thighs (skin on and on the bone)

1 ripe avocado

1 small red onion (very finely diced)

4 tbsp mayonnaise

A good slosh of Chillish® oil

2 tbsp Chillish® Just the Gubbins

A handful of chives (chopped)

A handful of rocket leaves

2 tortilla wraps or pitta bread

A few good crunches of salt and black pepper

METHOD:

1. Preheat the oven to 200°C.

2. Place chicken thighs in an oven proof dish and toss in the Chillish® oil, so they are nicely coated.

3. Roast (skin side up) for about 40 minutes (or until the meat is falling off the bone).

4. Meanwhile, in a bowl, add the avocado, red onion, mayonnaise, Chillish® Just the Gubbins, the chives and the rocket leaves. Season to taste. Mix together. Set aside.

5. When the chicken is ready, pull the quality meat from the bones and add any crispy skin. Add to the avocado mix.

6. Lightly heat the bread in the hot oven.

7. Divide the mixture between the two and serve immediately.

BEEF

RICH COTTAGE PIE

with a Chillish® Just the Gubbins & Garlish® Just the Crush Mash

This is a rich and punchy cottage pie, bursting with flavour. When I was at school, the cottage pie was always grim. The meat was chewy, the potatoes were pale and sloppy and I could never understand how with such basic ingredients, it could turn out so badly. So I hereby introduce you to my 'pimped' version. You can serve it in one big ovenproof dish, but if you want to show off, you can make individual dishes.

Serves: 4 people

INGREDIENTS:

A good slosh of Chillish® or Garlish® oil

800g best quality minced beef

1 large onion (finely diced)

1 carrot (finely diced)

200g petit pois peas (defrosted)

2 tbsp Garlish® Just the Crush

2 bay leaves

1 tbsp fresh thyme leaves

10 good shakes of Worcestershire sauce

1 (heaped) tbsp plain flour

2 tbsp tomato purée

200ml red port (red wine can be substituted)

1 beef stock cube (crumbled)

1 tsp salt

A few good grinds of black pepper

For the mash:

750g King Edward or Maris Piper potatoes (peeled and diced)

3 tbsp Chillish® Just the Gubbins

2 tbsp Garlish® Just the Crush

25g butter

30mls double cream

METHOD:

1. Preheat the oven to 200°C.
2. In a large pan, add the potatoes and a large pinch of salt. Cover with water and bring to the boil. Lower the heat slightly and leave to cook for 20 minutes (until soft). Once soft, drain and set aside.
3. Meanwhile, in a saucepan, on a high heat, add a slosh of oil, followed by the beef mince. Fry for 5 minutes until browned, then add the Worcestershire sauce. Fry for a further minute then remove the beef from the pan and set aside.
4. Add another slosh of oil to the pan and add the onion, carrot, thyme and bay leaves. Fry on a medium heat until the onions have softened (about 10mins).
5. Add the mince back into the pan, along with the flour, tomato purée and beef stock cube. Mix well and turn up the heat.
6. Add the port (or red wine) and bring to the boil, stirring continuously.
7. After a minute, turn the heat down and add the peas, Garlish® Just the Crush and season generously with salt and pepper. Simmer (with the lid off) for 45 minutes, stirring occasionally.
8. Meanwhile, add the butter, cream, Garlish® Just the Crush and Chillish® Just the Gubbins to the cooked potatoes. Mash together until there are no lumps.
9. Once the pie mixture is cooked, remove the bay leaves and spoon it into an ovenproof dish. Next, spread the potato mixture on top and with a fork, gently smooth over, making fork track marks as you go. Season with black pepper, then place in the oven for 30 minutes.

45

FILLET STEAK

with a Garlish® Mushroom & Truffle Sauce

Now this is a sauce that shoots the lights out – every time. You can make this recipe with any cut of beef. My husband prefers the flavour of a sirloin, but I love the tenderness of a fillet. The rich sauce compliments a less fatty cut, so for this I would recommend sticking with a fillet. Most important of all – you MUST let the meat rest after cooking. Always make sure it is room temperature before cooking…and get a thick good quality cut!

Serves: 2 people

INGREDIENTS:

300g x 2 fillet steak

250g chestnut mushrooms (sliced)

75g butter

100ml brandy

A good slosh of Garlish® oil

2 tbsp tomato purée

1 tbsp plain flour

1 tbsp Dijon mustard

2 tbsp Garlish® Just the Crush

A few good shakes of Worcestershire sauce

120ml double cream,

1 beef stock cube (crumbled)

A handful of parsley (chopped)

2 tbsp truffle oil

Salt and pepper

METHOD:

1. Season the steaks with salt and pepper – set aside.

2. In a frying pan, add the Garlish® oil and fry the mushrooms until they and brown and wilted. Remove with a slotted spoon and set aside.

3. Turn the heat up high and add the butter. Once it is bubbling, add the steaks.

4. Turn every minute for 5 minutes (or longer, depending on your preference). Set aside, cover in foil and a couple of tea towels. Leave to rest for 20 minutes.

5. Lower the heat and re-add the mushrooms and stir in the flour. Add the Worcestershire sauce and stir well. Turn the heat up high and add the brandy and stock cube. Bring to the boil, stirring continuously for 1 minute.

6. Turn the heat down low, then add the tomato purée, mustard, Garlish® Just the Crush, cream and truffle oil. Simmer gently for 5 minutes.

7. Stir through the chopped parsley.

8. When the steaks have rested, place them on a warm plate and pour over the sauce.

Serve immediately.

47

CHILLISH® JUST THE GUBBINS CON CARNE

with Garlish® Just the Crush Soured Cream

Chillish® Just the Gubbins really compliments this recipe. The sweet, smokiness adds such a depth of flavour. Please be sure to use the best quality mince that you can. You can add more or less Chillish® Just the Gubbins depending on how hot you like your food. Simply serve on a bed of fluffy white Basmati rice and a large dollop of Garlish® Just the Crush soured cream. Easy peasy!

Serves: 4 people

INGREDIENTS:

500g lean beef mince

2 tbsp Chillish® Just the Gubbins

400g can of red kidney beans

1 large onion (finely diced)

2 tbsp Garlish® Just the Crush

1 large red pepper (cut into strips)

1 tbsp paprika

A good slosh of Garlish® or Chillish® oil

3 tbsp tomato purée

2 tsp salt

A few good grinds of black pepper

1 tbsp flour

150ml red wine or port

1 beef stock cube (crumbled)

A large handful of fresh basil leaves (save 4 leaves for garnish).

200g soured cream

2 tbsp Garlish® Just the Crush

Salt and pepper

METHOD:

1.   On a high heat, add the oil to a pan and fry the mince. Season well with salt and pepper. When browned, remove from the pan and set aside to rest. Lower the heat and add another slosh of oil and add the diced onion. Cook until the onions are nicely browned and sweet smelling.

2.   Add the mince back into the pan and stir in the flour and paprika. Add the tomato purée, stock cube and red wine. Turn the heat up and stir continuously for 1 minute.

3.   Lower the heat and stir in the Chillish® Just the Gubbins and Garlish® Just the Crush.

4.   Simmer on a low heat for 45 minutes covering loosely with a lid. After 20 minutes, add the red pepper, drained kidney beans and chopped basil. Leave to reset for 5 minutes, then serve.

5.   To make the Garlish® soured cream: Simply mix the soured cream and Garlish® Just the Crush together, season to taste, then serve.

49

SPICY BEEF RENDANG
with Sticky Coconut & Star Anise

This is a rich, gooey, sticky and ultimately delicious Indonesian dish. Fresh ingredients are so important and you can usually find them in any international supermarket or even some of the bigger supermarkets. Serve with fluffy Jasmine rice.

Serves: 4 people

INGREDIENTS:
800g stewing beef (diced)
A good slosh of Garlish® oil
3 large round shallots (finely chopped)
160ml coconut cream
2 tbsp brown sugar
10 heaped tbsp desiccated coconut
4 tbsp fish sauce
A handful of coriander leaves

SPICE MIX A
2 cinnamon sticks
8 kaffir lime leaves (finely sliced)
6 cloves
4 star anise
4 cardamom pods (smashed)

SPICE MIX B
6 dried Kashmiri chillies (save one for garnish)

These ingredients need to be blended:
3 lemongrass sticks (topped and tailed)
3 inches of ginger
3 (heaped) tbsp Garlish® Just the Crush
2 tsp salt

METHOD:
1. Preheat oven to 160°C.
2. In a pan, add a splash of oil and fry the shallots and **SPICE MIX A**. Fry on a medium heat for 5-10 minutes until the shallots start to smell sweet.
3. Blend **SPICE MIX B** into a smooth paste and add to the pan. Reduce the heat and gently fry for 5 minutes.
4. Add the beef, chillies and coconut cream and mix well.
5. In another pan, dry fry the desiccated coconut on a high heat, tossing them until they turn a deep golden colour. Make sure they do not burn!
6. Once browned, add the coconut, fish sauce, sugar and coriander leaves. Place in the oven for 2 hours. After this time, remove the lid and cook uncovered for a further 20 minutes.
7. Remove from the oven and leave to rest for 20 minutes. Before serving, garnish with a few coriander leaves and a dried Kashmiri chilli.

CRISPY CHILLISH® JUST THE GUBBINS SIRLOIN BEEF STIR-FRY
with Ginger & Soy

Not only is this a very quick and satisfying meal, it is also utterly delicious. The cashew nuts give it that extra special something. I also love to eat this with chopsticks as it makes me feel like I am having a true Asian experience. A fork however, does the job.

Serves: 4 people

INGREDIENTS:

500g sirloin steak (thinly sliced)

1 egg (beaten)

2 tbsp dark soy sauce

200g plain flour

A VERY good slosh of Garlish® oil

1 onion (finely diced)

2 red peppers (sliced)

1 tbsp Garlish® Just the Crush

1 tbsp Chillish® Just the Gubbins

100ml soy sauce

4 tbsp honey

2 tbsp oyster sauce

500g vermicelli noodles

2 handfuls of cashew nuts

Sliced spring onions to serve

METHOD:

1. Place the beef strips in a bowl and add the soy sauce and egg. Set aside.

2. In a pan, add the oil, followed by the onions and red peppers. Fry on a medium – high temperature, until the onions have browned and the pepper is soft but firm.

3. Add the honey, soy sauce and oyster sauce.

4. Bring to the boil, then lower the heat to a gentle simmer.

5. Meanwhile, prepare the steak strips. Decant the flour onto a plate, then drain the soy from each strip and coat each one in flour.

6. In another frying pan, add a generous slosh of oil and when piping hot, add the strips, turning regularly. Fry until they are crispy and browned. Remove and place onto kitchen paper.

7. Cook the noodles as per the instructions, then drain. Add to the sauce, followed by the beef, spring onions, Garlish® Just the Crush and Chillish® Just the Gubbins and mix well. Add the Cashew nuts.

Serve immediately.

53

LAMB

SLOW COOKED LAMB SHOULDER
with A Garlish® Pistachio & Parsley Pistou

If you like lamb, you'll love this. A Pistou is something I came across many years ago in a restaurant in France. I was a little spun out by its appearance and was convinced that it was 'pesto' spelt wrong, but once I tasted it, I knew that I had to recreate it.

Serves: 4 people

INGREDIENTS:
1 x lamb shoulder 1.5 – 2 kg
1 onion (quartered)
5 garlic cloves
1 cinnamon stick

Marinade:
1 onion
A good slosh of Garlish® oil
A handful of rosemary leaves
A handful of thyme leaves
3 tbsp – Garlish® Just the Crush
2 tbsp mustard

1 tsp ground coriander
1 tsp cinnamon powder
Salt and pepper

Parsley Pistou:
2 large handfuls of fresh parsley
150g salted pistachios
3 tbsp Garlish® Just the Crush
1 tsp salt
1 tsp black pepper
100ml olive oil
Juice from 1 large orange

METHOD:
1. Place the leg of lamb in a roasting dish and using a very sharp knife, make plenty of holes in the meat.
2. Next, blend the marinade, then pour over the leg, making sure to push it down into the holes. Cover the dish and leave to marinade for 4-5 hours.
3. Once marinated, preheat the oven to 120°C. Add the onion quarters and garlic cloves to the dish and sprinkle the lamb with the rosemary. Add the cinnamon powder. Drizzle with oil and season generously with salt and pepper.
4. Cover with foil and place in the oven for 5 hours, or until the meat falls off the bone. Every hour, re-baste the lamb and jostle the onions and garlic in the oil.
5. When the lamb is ready, set aside, re-cover with foil and leave to stand for 30 minutes.
6. Meanwhile, in a saucepan on a medium heat, add the stock cube and add any juice from the resting lamb. Add the flour and bash out any lumps. Add the wine and the redcurrant jelly. bring to the boil, stirring continuously, for 1 minute, then lower the heat to a simmer.

For the Parsley Pistou:
1. Simply blend the ingredients together. The mixture should be like a paste, so if it runs too thick, simply add more olive oil or orange juice.
2. Once ready to serve, roughly pull the meat apart and drizzle over the gravy. Add the roasted garlic cloves and onions. Serve with the Pistou on the side.

GARLISH® LEG OF LAMB
with Rosemary, Orange & Fennel

This is a spectacular recipe which I make time and time again. The Garlish® Just the Crush wildly complements the lamb and the key is to get as much of it into the incisions as possible. The flavours will permeate through the meat, giving an overall outstanding flavour. It is also very easy to make and can be carved at the table.

Serves: 4 people

INGREDIENTS:

3 tbsp Just the Garlish® Just the Crush

1 leg of lamb (approx. 1.8kg – room temperature)

A good slosh of Garlish® oil

25g salted butter

A handful of rosemary leaves

3 tbsp fennel seeds (bashed)

Zest and juice from 2 oranges

1 tsp salt

A few good grinds of black pepper

Gravy:

Lamb stock cube

1 tbsp plain flour

2 tsp redcurrant jelly

2 tbsp Worcestershire sauce

100ml port (or red wine)

METHOD:

1. Preheat the oven to 160°C.

2. Generously season the lamb with salt and pepper.

3. In a large frying pan, add the oil and butter and on a high heat, brown the lamb all over for 5 minutes.

4. Place the Lamb on a baking tray and make a number of incisions all over. Pack the holes with the Garlish® Just the Crush, then zest and squeeze the oranges and sprinkle/drizzle both over the top, ensuring as much goes in to the holes as possible.

5. Bash the rosemary and thyme leaves in a pestle and mortar, then sprinkle over the lamb.

6. Place in the oven for 1hr, basting every 20 minutes.

7. Remove from the oven, cover in foil and set aside to rest for 30 minutes. Cover the foil with a couple of tea towels to keep the heat in.

8. Meanwhile, in a pan, add the flour and stock cube. Add the juices from the resting lamb and stir in the port. Bring to the boil for 1 minute. Lower the heat and stir in the Worcestershire sauce and redcurrant jelly. Season to taste.

Serve immediately.

LAMB KOFTAS

with a Gubbins® Greek Yoghurt dressing

These make a fabulous lunch. I make them in batches and keep them in the fridge so they are easily accessible. If I have time, I skewer them but you can shape them however you wish. They also make lovely patties! You can serve them with flatbreads, rice or even just with a side salad.

Makes: 8 Skewers

INGREDIENTS:

A slosh of Garlish® oil

Kofta mix:

500g best quality lamb mince

1 onion (grated)

1 tbsp Garlish® Just the Crush

2 handfuls of flat leaf parsley (finely chopped)

1 handful of fresh mint leaves (finely chopped)

1 handful of fresh coriander leaves (finely chopped)

1 handful of coarse breadcrumbs

2 tsp ground cumin

2 tsp ground coriander

½ tsp ground cinnamon

1 tsp allspice

2 tsp paprika

2 tsp salt

A few good grinds of black pepper

The dressing:

2 tbsp Chillish® Just the Gubbins

500g Greek yoghurt

1 tsp cumin

1 tbsp lemon Juice

Salt and pepper

METHOD:

1. In a bowl, mix together the dressing ingredients and place in the fridge.

2. If you are using wooden skewers, soak these in water on a large plate.

3. In a large bowl, add the **kofta mix** ingredients and using your hands, mix it all together until it resembles a smooth but firm paste. If the mixture seems too wet, then add a sprinkle of breadcrumbs.

4. Dry the skewers and shape a handful of the mixture around each one.

5. In a large frying pan, add the Garlish® oil and turn the heat up high. Add the skewers in batches, turning regularly, until browned. Remove from the heat and cover with foil. Leave to rest for 10 minutes.

Serve immediately.

LAMB MOUSSAKA

with a Garlish® Béchamel Sauce

This is such a beautiful dish. It's not the most straight forward of recipes and will require a bit of extra washing up, but it is well worth it. It is paramount that the aubergines are cooked properly, otherwise they will be too firm and tasteless. Make it once and you'll make it again and again.

Serves: 4 people

INGREDIENTS:
500g best quality lamb mince
1 onion (finely chopped)
2 tbsp Garlish® Just the Crush
A few good sloshes of Garlish® oil
2 tsp dried oregano
2 tsp dried mint
2 bay leaves
½ tsp cinnamon powder
1 tbsp plain flour
200ml red wine
400g tin chopped tomatoes
2 tbsp tomato purée

2 aubergines (thinly sliced)
1 lamb stock cube (crumbled)
6 medium Kind Edward potatoes (peeled and sliced)

The Béchamel sauce:
50g butter
50g flour
2 tbsp Garlish® Just the Crush
400ml whole milk
50g Parmesan (grated)
1 tsp finely grated nutmeg
Salt and pepper

METHOD:
1. Preheat the oven to 180°C.
2. In a large pan, add the Garlish® oil and turn up the heat. Add the lamb and fry for 5 minutes until it has browned. Remove with a slotted spoon and set aside.
3. In the same pan, add the onion and fry until translucent and soft. Add the lamb back into the pan, followed by the oregano, cinnamon, mint and bay leaves. Cook for a further 8-10 minutes.
4. Season generously with salt and pepper, then stir in the flour. Turn up the heat and add the wine. Cook for one minute, then add the tinned tomatoes, tomato purée, lamb stock cube and Garlish® Just the Crush. Stir well then leave to gently simmer.
5. In another large frying pan, add more oil and fry the sliced aubergine in batches. Once they have softened and browned remove and place on kitchen paper.
6. Bring a saucepan of water to the boil and add a tsp of salt. Add the sliced potatoes and boil for 5-8 minutes. Drain and set aside.
7. To make the **Béchamel sauce**, melt the butter in a saucepan then stir in the flour. Slowly pour in the milk, followed by the nutmeg and half of the Parmesan. Leave to lightly simmer for two minutes, then add the Garlish® Just the Crush. Season to taste.
8. In an ovenproof dish, add 1/3 of the lamb, followed by 1/3 of the potatoes, followed by 1/3 of the aubergines. Repeat the layers, finishing with aubergine.
9. Pour over the Béchamel sauce, pushing it between the gaps, then sprinkle with the remaining Parmesan. Place in the oven for 50 minutes.
10. Leave to stand for 10 minutes, before serving.

IRISH STEW

with Guinness® & Pearl Barley

Irish stew has to be one of my favourites. Lamb neck is wonderfully tender and the richness from the Guinness® adds such hearty depth. This is one of those dishes that will always taste better the next day as the potatoes and meat have had that extra time to absorb the magnificent flavours.

Serves: 4 people

INGREDIENTS:

5 rashers of smoked streaky bacon (cut into small pieces)

400g lamb neck (cut into chunks)

A slosh of Garlish® oil

2 tbsp Garlish® Just the Crush

5 medium King Edward potatoes (peeled and halved)

500ml Guinness®

2 medium carrots (cut into chunks)

Knob of butter

2 onions (diced)

2 bay leaves

1 tbsp of plain flour

½ tsp nutmeg

A handful of thyme leaves

2 tbsp pearl barley

500ml lamb stock

Parsley (chopped)

Salt and pepper

METHOD:

1. Preheat the oven to 140°C.

2. In a large frying pan, add the Garlish® oil and turn up the heat. Add the bacon pieces and fry until they are crispy. Remove from the pan and set aside.

3. Coat the lamb chunks in the flour and season well. Again, on a high heat, fry the lamb on all sides until it has browned. Lower the heat, then remove from the pan.

4. Add a knob of butter to the pan and on a medium heat fry the onions and carrots. Once the onions are soft, add the thyme leaves, bay leaves and nutmeg. Stir in the pearl barley.

5. Add the Guinness® and lamb stock and bring to the boil for 1 minute. Lower the heat and add the lamb and bacon back to the pan. Add the Garlish® Just the Crush. Stir well, then decant into an ovenproof dish.

6. Submerge the potatoes on top of the dish and season well. Cover the dish and place in the oven for 2 hours. Once cooked, let it stand for 20 minutes before serving. Garnish with chopped parsley.

SEAFOOD

CREAMY GARLISH® AND TIGER PRAWN LINGUINE
with Sundried Tomatoes & Parsley

This quick recipe is simply outstanding. So why did I choose linguine over spaghetti? Well quite frankly, its simple. Linguine (due to its flat shape and greater surface area) holds onto sauces better. It also sounds rather snazzy. I always have linguini in the cupboard and I always have prawns in the freezer.

Serves: 4 people

INGREDIENTS:

A slosh of Garlish® oil

300g linguine pasta (fresh if possible)

300g large prawns (uncooked)

10 sundried tomatoes (finely chopped)

4 (heaped) tbsp Garlish® Just the Crush

A large handful of parsley (finely chopped)

Juice of 1 lemon

150g single cream

2 tsp salt

2 tsp ground black pepper

1 tbsp tomato purée

METHOD:

1. Boil the linguine in salted water as per the instructions. Set aside.

2. Meanwhile, in a large wok or pan, add the Garlish® oil and fry the prawns on a medium heat for 3 minutes or until cooked through.

3. Add the cooked linguine, lemon juice and Garlish® Just the Crush, then lower the heat and add the cream, tomato purée, parsley, sundried tomatoes, salt and pepper.

Serve immediately.

THE ULTIMATE:
CONDIMENT
MARINADE
DRIZZLER
DIP
OIL

Chef

SEARED COD

with a Garlish® & Lemon Sauce

Cod is a stunning fish. I use it in this recipe because it has a fabulous texture and a wonderfully mild and milky flavour. There is something about garlic and fish together that just screams 'holiday by the sea'. This is so delicious and so easy to make, it really takes no time at all.

Serves: 2 people

INGREDIENTS:

2 x cod loins

A slosh of Garlish® oil

25g butter

2 tbsp Garlish® Just the Crush

Juice of 1 lemon

A handful of fresh chives (finely chopped)

Salt and pepper

METHOD:

1. In a frying pan, add the butter and a slosh of the Garlish® oil. Turn the heat up high, then add the cod. Sear in the pan for 3 minutes each side or until cooked. Remove from the pan and generously season with salt and pepper. Set aside to rest under foil for 5 minutes.

2. Meanwhile, lower the heat and add the Garlish® Just the Crush, chives and lemon juice and gently warm through.

3. Place the cod on each plate and spoon over the sauce.

Serve immediately.

SIDE OF SALMON

with an Orange & Pomegranate Glaze

Not only is this dish easy on the eye, with its lavish colours, but it also tastes utterly incredible. I always think of pomegranate seeds as 'jewels'. The key to this recipe is to reduce the glaze down so it is thick enough to spread over the salmon. I would serve this straight from the oven and let everyone spoon it straight from the dish.

Serves: 4 people

INGREDIENTS:

1 large side of salmon

Zest and juice from 4 oranges plus one sliced

100ml pomegranate juice

A large handful of pomegranate seeds (drained)

3 tbsp honey

1 tbsp brown sugar

1 tbsp Garlish® Just the Crush

METHOD:

1. Preheat the oven to 160°C.

2. Place the salmon (skin side down), in an oven dish. Set aside.

3. Add the orange zest, orange juice, pomegranate juice and honey to a saucepan and bring to the boil, then turn down the heat and simmer for 10 or so minutes until it is thick and syrupy.

4. Sprinkle the sugar over the orange slices.

5. In frying pan, on a medium – high heat, add a slosh of Garlish® oil followed by the orange slices. Fry until soft and browned. Set aside.

6. Once the glaze is ready, stir in the Garlish® Just the Crush, then spread over the salmon. Arrange the orange slices on the top.

7. Place in the oven for 15 – 20 minutes, until just cooked. Leave to rest for 5 minutes then sprinkle over the pomegranate seeds.

Serve immediately.

SMOKED HADDOCK CHOWDER

I had my first Chowder in San Francisco back in 2009. I had never had one before but I will never forget it. It was so rich, warming and dreamy. I knew from that moment that I had to recreate it…and I have done just that.

Serves: 4 people

INGREDIENTS:

500g smoked haddock

5 medium potatoes (peeled and diced)

5 rashers of smoked streaky bacon (chopped)

A slosh of Garlish® oil

1 tbsp Garlish® Just the Crush

1 onion (diced)

1 leek (sliced)

2 celery sticks (sliced)

50g butter

A handful of sweetcorn

2 bay leaves

1tsp smoked paprika

100ml fish stock

100ml single cream

A handful of fresh thyme (chopped)

500ml milk

A handful of fresh parsley (finely chopped)

Salt and pepper

METHOD:

1. In a pan, add the haddock, milk and bay leaves. Bring to the boil then reduce to a simmer. Cook for 5 minutes until it is just cooked. Set aside.

2. In another pan, add the Garlish® oil and fry the bacon until crispy (remove a few pieces for garnish). Next, add the butter, onions, leeks, celery, thyme and paprika. Fry for 5 minutes on a medium heat.

3. Add the potatoes and season generously with salt and pepper.

4. Meanwhile, drain the milk from the haddock and add it to the pan along with the fish stock. Bring to the boil then put the lid on and lower the heat to a simmer. Stir every 5 minutes and leave to cook for 25 minutes, until the potatoes are soft and falling apart. Blend in a food processor, then return back to the pan.

5. Check the haddock for bones / skin then gently flake it and add to the pan. Stir in the cream, parsley and Garlish® Just the Crush, then season to taste. Heat through then ladle into individual bowls and sprinkle over the sweetcorn and the remaining bacon pieces.

Serve immediately.

SPICY CALAMARI & PRAWN PAELLA

with Chillish® Just the Gubbins and Chorizo

Paella is a wonderful dish and lends itself beautifully to chilli and garlic. One key thing to remember with Paella, is not to stir it too much once it has started to cook. If the stock runs out and the rice is still uncooked, just add a little more stock.

Serves: 4 people

INGREDIENTS:

4 skinless and boneless chicken thighs (diced)

200g raw king prawns

180g calamari rings

12 slices of chorizo

300g paella rice

A slosh of Garlish® oil

1 onion (finely diced)

2 tbsp Garlish® Just the Crush

100ml dry white wine

1 tbsp Chillish® Just the Gubbins

1 tsp turmeric

A handful of petit pois peas (frozen)

1 tbsp smoked paprika

700mls fish stock (hot)

A handful of chopped parsley

Salt and pepper

1 lemon (quartered – for garnish)

METHOD:

1. Heat the Garlish® oil in a large pan and add the diced chicken and chorizo. Fry until the chicken has browned and the chorizo is crispy. Remove with a slotted spoon and set aside.

2. Turn the heat down, add a little more oil and fry the onions until they are soft and brown.

3. Add the turmeric, paprika, Chillish® Just the Gubbins and Garlish® Just the Crush, then add the rice and mix together well. Generously season with salt and black pepper. Fry for 2 minutes.

4. Next, add the white wine and bring to the boil (uncovered). Lower the heat to a simmer, then over the next 15 - 20 minutes, add the fish stock in stages. After 10 minutes into this process, add the prawns, calamari and peas to the surface (do not stir them into the rice).

5. Once the rice, prawns and calamari are cooked, cover the dish in foil and leave to stand for 10 minutes.

6. Garnish with chopped parsley and lemon wedges.

Serve immediately.

VEGETARIAN

CRISPY SESAME & HONEY TOFU

with a Chillish® Sweet Potato Rosti

Tofu is a wonderful invention, but you have to get it right. You must ensure that as much water as possible has been extracted before cooking, otherwise it will be soggy.

Serves: 2 people

INGREDIENTS:

500g extra firm tofu

3 tbsp corn starch

A good slosh of sesame oil

A good slosh of Garlish® oil

5 tbsp soy sauce

2 tbsp honey

1 tbsp Garlish® Just the Crush

A handful of black sesame seeds

For the Rosti:

4 small sweet potatoes (thick grated)

A good slosh of Chillish® oil

1 tbsp Chillish® Just the Gubbins

1 onion (grated)

2 tsp salt

2 tsp pepper

2 tbsp flour

A handful of chives (chopped)

Salt and pepper

METHOD:

1. Preheat the oven to 140°C.

2. Drain the tofu and wrap tightly in kitchen paper. Place a heavy pan/item on top and leave for 20 minutes to drain as much water as possible. Change the paper towels every 5 minutes or as needed.

3. Place the grated sweet potato and onion onto a clean tea towel and wring together so as to discard any water. Place into a bowl and add the flour, chives, Chillish® Just the Gubbins, egg, salt and pepper. Mix well.

4. Once the Tofu is ready, cube it into small chunks and place into a bowl. Add the cornstarch and ensure each cube is well coated. Set aside.

5. On a medium-high heat, add the Chillish® oil to the pan. Take a handful of rosti mixture and shape it into a tight ball, then pat it in to a round circle (approximately 1 cm thick). Add to the oil and fry each one (in batches) for about 8-10 minutes being careful not to burn them. Once they are cooked through and crispy, place them in the oven to keep warm.

6. Now for the tofu. Turn up the heat and add the Garlish® oil and sesame oil. Once it is starting to bubble, add the tofu. With a fork, gently turn them so all sides are browned and crispy. This should take 5 -10 minutes.

7. Once browned, lower the heat and add the soy sauce, honey, sesame seeds and Garlish® Just the Crush. Stir well and cook for 2 minutes. Remove from the heat and serve alongside the Rosti's.

VEGAN

ROASTED VEGETABLE COUSCOUS
with Shallots, Courgettes & Chillish®

Couscous is such a beautiful thing. Technically it is a pasta (made with crushed durham wheat semolina), but it is very different in texture. I always choose wholegrain as it is firmer, nuttier and allround healthier. Roasted vegetables compliment it beautifully. I sometimes make this as an accompaniment to a larger meal and works very well on a buffet table served cold. You can't go wrong, it is truly delicious.

Serves: 4 people

INGREDIENTS:

200g wholegrain couscous

200ml vegetable stock

A good slosh of Chillish® oil

10 small shallots (peeled and halved)

2 medium courgettes (sliced)

1 red pepper (sliced)

1 yellow pepper (sliced)

A handful parsley (chopped)

3 tbsp tomato purée

Salt and pepper

METHOD:

1.   Preheat the oven to 160°C.

2.   In an oven dish, add the courgette, aubergine, peppers and shallots and generously coat in the Chillish® oil. Season with salt and pepper. Cook for 40 minutes, re-basting in the oil every 15 minutes.

3.   Meanwhile, in a saucepan, bring the vegetable stock to the boil, then add the couscous. Place the lid on and remove from the heat. Set aside undisturbed until the vegetables are ready.

4.   When the vegetables are soft and gooey, add a little more oil, tomato purée and parsley to the tray. Mix well and heat through for 5 minutes, then combine with the couscous. Then place in the oven for 5 minutes to warm through.

PEAR, GOATS CHEESE & POMEGRANATE SALAD
with Chillish® roasted Butternut

Pear and goats cheese make a wonderful marriage. Add in the sweet and tart pomegranate seeds and it takes it to another level. Whenever I make a salad, I always chop the green leaves into tiny pieces (with scissors) so as to cram more in (to meet my 5 a day!). Just a tip.

Serves: 4 people

INGREDIENTS:

A good slosh of Chillish® oil

1 butternut squash (deseeded and cubed)

200g dark green salad leaves

2 ripe pears (sliced lengthways)

200g goats cheese (crumbled)

200g pomegranate seeds

3 handfuls of walnuts

The dressing:

A good slosh of Garlish® oil

2 tbsp Dijon mustard

2 tbsp white wine or sherry vinegar

3 tbsp honey

Salt and pepper

METHOD:

1.   Preheat the oven to 160°C.

2.   Wash the butternut under warm water to clean the skin, then cut it into 1cm squares. Discard the stringy flesh and seeds. Place in an ovenproof dish and coat in the Chillish® oil. Season well with salt and pepper and place in the oven. Cook for 45 minutes until soft and crispy.

3.   Meanwhile, build each salad. In each bowl, layer the green salad leaves, followed by the pears, goats cheese, pomegranate seeds and walnuts.

4.   Mix together the dressing ingredients and set aside.

5.   Once the butternut squash is ready, add to each salad, then drizzle over the dressing.

GORGONZOLA & SPINACH PENNE
with Chillish® Walnuts

Wow. Now this is a stunning recipe. It is rather indulgent and you certainly don't need a huge portion as it is rather rich, but the flavours are simply outstanding. For me, it ticks every box.

Serves: 4 people

INGREDIENTS:

400g penne pasta

2 tbsp butter

2 tbsp Garlish® Just the Crush

150 ml single cream

125g Gorgonzola cheese (crumbled)

2 tbsp Parmesan (grated)

3 tbsp fresh parsley (chopped)

1 large handful of spinach leaves

1 tsp salt

A few grinds of black pepper

2 handfuls of walnuts (chopped)

1 tbsp Chillish® Just the Gubbins

METHOD:

1. Bring a pan of water to the boil and add the penne. Cook as per the instructions. Once cooked, drain and set aside.

2. Meanwhile, melt the butter in a pan over a medium heat and add the spinach, cream, Garlish® Just the Crush, Gorgonzola, parsley, salt and pepper. Leave to gently simmer.

3. In a separate pan, on a medium heat, add the walnuts. Once they start to brown, add the Chillish® Just the Gubbins. Mix well and then remove from the heat.

4. Mix the cheese sauce into the cooked pasta. Serve into warm bowls and sprinkle with the walnuts and Parmesan.

Serve immediately.

CRISPY GARLISH® & CHILLISH® GNOCCHI
with Basil and Parmesan

This is a quick recipe and tastes just fantastic. To make this dish Vegan, simply choose a Vegan brand of Gnocchi and substitute the Parmesan cheese.

Serves: 2 people

INGREDIENTS:

3 tbsp Garlish® Just the Crush

1 tbsp Chillish® Just the Gubbins

500g gnocchi

A good slosh of Garlish® or Chillish® oil

A large handful of basil (finely chopped and a handful kept aside for garnish)

1 tsp red wine vinegar

200g passata

1 tsp salt

3 tbsp Parmesan

A few grinds of black pepper

METHOD:

1. Add a generous slosh of oil to a frying pan and turn the heat up high. Add the gnocchi and fry for 5 minutes, or until crispy.

2. Lower the heat, then add the add the red wine vinegar, passata, Garlish® Just the Crush, Chillish® Just the Gubbins and basil. Season generously with salt and pepper and simmer for 10 minutes.

3. Serve with a sprinkle of Parmesan and remaining basil.

Serve immediately.

89

SIDES

SPICY TENDERSTEM® BROCCOLI

This is such an easy recipe and takes no time at all. I have eaten this on its own a number of times! I only ever use Tenderstem® broccoli because it has a wonderful crunch and I always think of it as a hybrid of asparagus and kale. Both of which I love.

Serves: 4 people

INGREDIENTS:

400g Tenderstem® broccoli
1 tbsp Chillish® Just the Gubbins

5 tbsp Chillish® oil
2 tbsp grated Parmesan cheese

METHOD:

1. Add the Chillish® oil to a pan and turn the heat up to medium-high. Add the broccoli and coat in the oil. Fry for 5-6 minutes until just cooked.

2. Lower the heat and stir in the Chillish® Just the Gubbins. Arrange the broccoli on a plate and sprinkle over the grated Parmesan.

Serve immediately.

GARLISH® SAUTÉED SPINACH

This is a fabulous accompaniment to almost any main course. Please make sure you wash the leaves thoroughly before cooking or buy pre-washed leaves. You will be amazed at how much the spinach shrinks, so please don't be alarmed by the initial volume!

Serves: 4 people

INGREDIENTS:

520g spinach leaves (chopped)
3 tbsp Garlish® oil
3 tbsp Garlish® Just the Crush

A knob of butter
2 tbsp double cream
A few grinds of black pepper

METHOD:

1. In a large frying pan, add the Garlish® oil and butter and then increase the heat to medium-high. Add the chopped spinach in batches. Keep going until eventually the leaves have dramatically reduced in size.

2. Keep tossing the leaves until they start to crisp and there is no water (approximately 10 minutes). Lower the heat and add the Garlish® Just the Crush, cream and black pepper. Mix well.

Serve immediately.

GOLDEN ROASTED GARLISH® NEW POTATOES

Roast potatoes are one of life's biggest pleasures. Roasted baby potatoes however, take it to another level. Because they are literally that - a baby potato - they hold a huge amount of flavour. Roasting them gives you the best of both worlds. They also do not require peeling, which is a bonus.

Serves: 4 people

INGREDIENTS:

3 tbsp Garlish® oil

25g butter

750g baby potatoes

1 tbsp plain flour

2 tbsp Garlish® Just the Crush

3 tsp salt

A few grinds of black pepper

METHOD:

1.   Preheat the oven to 180°C.

2.   Boil the potatoes in salted water for 8 minutes, then drain well and set aside.

3.   In a large ovenproof dish, add the Garlish® oil and butter and place in the oven.

4.   After 5 minutes, remove the dish from the oven and add the potatoes, coating them in the oil and butter. Add the salt and pepper.

5.   Roast for 45-50 minutes, turning occasionally. Remove from the oven and add the Garlish® Just the Crush. Mix well.

Serve immediately.

CHILLISH® SWEET POTATO PURÉE

This is utterly delicious. I would recommend using a blender to get the right consistency. If it is too 'runny' you can add it back to the pan and gently simmer until some of the liquid evaporates.

Serves: 4 people

INGREDIENTS:

4 small sweet potatoes (peeled and diced)

2 tbsp Chillish® Just the Gubbins

50ml double cream

A handful of chives (chopped)

1 tsp salt

A few grinds of black pepper

METHOD:

1.   In a large pan, add the sweet potato and enough water to just cover. Add a teaspoon of salt and bring to the boil. Once soft, remove from the heat, drain well and set aside.

2.   Blend the sweet potato with the Chillish® Just the Gubbins and cream. Stir in the fresh chives and season to taste.

Serve immediately.

PUDDINGS

TOR'S ETON MESS

I absolutely love Eton Mess. The apparent reason for the name stems from a Pavlova being served at a cricket match between Eton and Harrow school many years ago. It was dropped just before service. Everyone was in a panic but someone suggested scooping it up in a crumpled mess and serving it...and owning the mistake and calling it Eton Mess. It's a great story but who knows if it is true. My special friend Tor, makes thee most incredible version, so I hereby give her the reigns to share her expertise.

Serves: 4 people

INGREDIENTS:

400g ripe strawberries (halved)

160g white sugar

600ml double cream

12 small meringue nests (6 roughly broken and) plus 4 kept whole

30ml of kirsch cherry liqueur (optional)

METHOD:

1. Whip the double cream in a mixing bowl until it forms soft peaks.

2. Blend half of the strawberries, Kirsch (if using) and sugar. Set aside.

3. Add the broken pieces of meringue to the whipped cream, followed by the strawberries and the strawberry purée, saving a little to drizzle over the finished piece.

4. Spoon into individual glasses or one large serving bowl. Place the remaining whole meringues on the top, then serve.

97

CLOTTED CREAM CHOCOLATE GANACHE AND ORANGE POTS

This is a truly remarkable pudding. It is rich and velvety and so incredibly easy to prepare, plus you can make it in advance. I use clotted cream because…well why not? If you ever mention clotted cream to someone with a sweet tooth, you'll almost always hear an 'ooooo'. It makes me laugh every time.

Serves: 4 people

INGREDIENTS:

220g plain chocolate

1 large (unwaxed) orange (zest plus 2 tbsp juice)

250g clotted cream

1 tsp vanilla paste

METHOD:

1. Grate 2 tbsp of the dark chocolate into a bowl, then zest 1 tbsp of orange into a second bowl. Place in the fridge.

2. Put all of the ingredients into a large heatproof bowl, then place over a saucepan of simmering water. Gently stir until it has melted.

3. Remove from the heat, then pour into serving glasses or ramekins. Allow to cool.

4. Place in the fridge and allow to set for 3 hours or overnight.

5. Before serving, sprinkle each pot with the grated chocolate and orange zest.

APPLE & RASPBERRY CRUMBLE

There is nothing like the smell of a crumble cooking. Its homely, fiercely British and incredibly easy to make. You can buy crumble topping if you want to speed things up and don't like getting your hands dirty. I always have a bag in the cupboard in case I need to whip one up at the drop of a hat. I always have apples in the fruit bowl and frozen berries in the freezer.

Serves: 4 people

INGREDIENTS:

4 Pink Lady apples (peeled, cored and cubed)

300g raspberries

25g butter

1 tsp flour

125g caster sugar

1 tbsp vanilla paste

½ tsp cinnamon powder

For the crumble:

230g plain flour

120g butter (cold and cubed)

100g demerara sugar

50g ground almonds

Cream or vanilla ice cream to serve

METHOD:

1. Preheat the oven to 180°C.

2. In a large pan, add the butter, followed by the apples and sugar. Sweat over a medium heat until they are soft. Add the vanilla paste, cinnamon, flour and raspberries. Cook for a further 2 minutes, then remove from the heat.

3. To make the **crumble topping**, place the flour into a mixing bowl, then add the butter. Mix together with your fingertips until it resembles a 'chunky sand'. Add the demerara sugar and ground almonds and mix well.

4. Place the filling into a baking dish, then spoon the crumble mixture on top. Place in the oven for 40-45 minutes, until the crumble is golden brown.

5. Remove from the oven and leave to rest for 5 minutes.

Serve with cream or vanilla ice cream.

STRAWBERRY CRÈME BRÛLÉE

Who doesn't love a Crème Brûlée? Who doesn't love strawberries?
Who doesn't love to tap the top of a Crème Brûlée and hear it crack? I am
guessing not many people. That's why this is a match made in heaven. You will
need a chef's torch to blast the sugar topping, but they are amazingly handy for
many recipes, so it is worth investing in one.

Serves: 4 people

INGREDIENTS:

500ml double cream

1 tsp vanilla paste

5 large egg yolks

60g caster sugar

60g demerara sugar

1 tbsp freeze dried strawberry powder

4 fresh strawberries (quatered)

METHOD:

1. Preheat oven to 160°C.

2. Add the cream and vanilla paste to a pan and bring to a near boil, then lower the heat and simmer for 2 minutes. Remove the heat and leave to cool.

3. In a bowl, whisk together the castor sugar and egg yolks for about 2 minutes, until they form a thick consistency. Whilst continuing to whisk, very slowly add the warm cream, followed by the strawberry powder.

4. Place the ramekins onto an oven tray, then pour in the mixture, followed by one quatered strawberry per portion. Add water to the tray, so it comes half way up the ramekins.

5. Bake for 25 minutes or until just set. Remove from the oven and set aside to cool completely. Cover each ramekin in clingfilm and place in the fridge for 5 hours.

6. Remove from the fridge, then sprinkle the demerara evenly over each ramekin, smoothing over with a spoon. Blast each one with a chef's torch until a hardened layer of crisp sugar forms.

THE ULTIMATE CHOCOLATE CHEESECAKE

Now, this my friends, is something in its own league. I love chocolate, but I am not interested in run of the mill 'chocolate'. I am wanting rich, decadent send-me-to-mars chocolate, hence why I created this masterpiece. I just wish it wasn't called 'cheesecake' as this gives the wrong impression as there is nothing cheesy about it!

INGREDIENTS:

For the biscuit base

450g dark chocolate Hobnob biscuits

150g butter

2 tbsp light brown sugar

1 tsp cocoa powder

For the cheesecake

450g dark chocolate pieces (plus 50g grated for decoration)

360ml double cream

3 tbsp cocoa powder

600g full-fat cream cheese

350g caster sugar

1tsp vanilla paste

METHOD:

1. Line a spring-based tin with parchment paper.

2. Blitz the Hobnobs in a food processor and pour them into a large bowl. Please note that you can also put them in a bag and bash them to smithereens with a rolling pin. Add the melted butter, sugar and cocoa and mix thoroughly.

3. Transfer the biscuit base mix to the tin. Using the back of a spoon, smooth over until it forms a firm, flat base. Refrigerate for 1 hour.

4. Place a heatproof bowl over a pan of simmering water, then add the chocolate pieces. Once melted, turn off the heat and set aside to cool.

5. In a large bowl, whip the cream until it forms soft peaks, then gently stir in the cocoa powder and vanilla paste.

6. In a second bowl, beat the sugar into the cream cheese. Add to the cream mixture and then slowly add the melted chocolate. Stir together well.

7. Pour over the chilled biscuit base and smooth over with a spatula, then sprinkle with the grated chocolate. Place in the fridge and chill overnight.

LEMON & LIME POSSET

The ultimate palate cleanser. This is such an easy recipe and can be made a day in advance. I love lemons, but I have always had a bit of a soft spot for limes. I guess because they slightly more tart which in my mind means more refreshing. Having said that, I have catered for that in this recipe and added just the right sweetness. I do still love lemons, hence why it is a hybrid.

Serves: 4 people

INGREDIENTS:

600ml double cream

200g caster Sugar

Zest and juice of 2 limes (unwaxed)

Zest and juice of 2 lemon (unwaxed)

1 tsp vanilla paste

METHOD:

1. Place the cream and sugar into a large pan and boil vigorously for 2 minutes, whilst stirring continuously.

2. Remove from the heat and stir in both the lemon and lime juice and zest (save a little zest to garnish), followed by the vanilla paste.

3. Leave to cool slightly, then divide the mixture into serving glasses. Once cool, place in the fridge for 3 hours or overnight.

4. Garnish with the remaining zest, then serve.

THANK YOU'S

First of all, I would like to say THANK YOU to YOU, for reading my book and for buying it. Thank you from the bottom of my heart. I know how much trust goes into creating something that someone else tells you is good, so thank you for trusting me.

Thank you to all of my current customers and amazing stockists.

MY HUSBAND – I could never have done this without your support, your encouragement and your love. Thank you for believing in me and pushing me to reach my goals. I hold a very special place in my heart for you. Thank you for being such a wonderful father to our children and looking after me so well. You are one of a kind.

MY MUM – the strongest and most powerful woman I know. A trooper and a fighter. Thank you for everything you have done to protect us and make us who we are. You are a true inspiration and I am so grateful to you. Don't ever change.

MICKEY – Thank you for always looking out for me and being such a wonderful stepfather.

MY SISTER – My sounding board and my best friend. Thank you for being such an incredible role model and always being there.

MY DAD – for always believing in me and holding me accountable from another world.

ESTELLE – Thank you for helping me with recipe ideas and helping with the boys so I could get my head down.

MY NEIGHBOURS – Paul and Kelly, Bob and Jane and Nick and Sue, for putting up with the endless lorries, skips, deliveries and feline escapes.

KATIE PHILLIPS – I could never have done this without your support. I will forever be grateful.

M-O-T-L – Thank you for our special times together. I can't wait for more. I love you. Always will.

TOR DRUMMOND-PARKER – Where do I start? Tor - you are just the sweetest creation and have helped me so much with Pollyanna's Kitchen. Thank you from the bottom of my heart.

LEAH BARR – Our very special bond formed after our trip in 2019 will never cease. You are amazing and I am so grateful to you. You are solid as a rock and I adore you.

JENNY KEMP-POTTER – my Thermomix lover! You are just amazing in every way. Thank you for the endless laughs. You are such a wholesome creature and you are so incredibly special to me.

DC SALLY DRURY-SMITH – Thank you for all of your support and keeping me updated with key information and for the endless laughs.

KATHRYN CRAGG – RUBY & WEBB CANDLES – for the laughs, fierce loyalty and allowing me to enjoy watching your business flourish. I am so proud of you!

CHRIS COOPER – SEOFON – for swallowing your words when I turned up with my original product (won't repeat the name). and you saw my determination and believed in my business. I truly thank you for all of your ongoing support.

KAREN HIBBART – FREELANCE DESIGN & GRAPHICS – Thank you for helping me create such a fabulous brand and always going above and beyond with designs and ideas.

KATIE KAZLAUCIUNAS – for helping me label my jars when my fingers hurt! You are amazing and I am so grateful for all of your help.

HEATHER JOY – JOY STARS – What a wonderful woman you are! Thank you for having my back and helping me spread my wings.

CATH LOWE – CATH LOWE PHOTOGRAPHY – for creating all of the pictures for this book! They were three of the most intense days ever, but I enjoyed them. Thank you for being so fabulous.

HELEN LEE & HELEN BEDFORD – you guys are the best! Thank you for looking after me and always going above and beyond. I couldn't work from home without you!

HARI HAROULLA – Thank you for your loyal friendship and helping me find my way in the early days.

MICHAEL & JEANETTE – for your fabulous ideas, feedback, menu-tasting and interest in my business.

COLIN & ADRIAN – HENNING'S WINE MERCHANTS – for supplying sensational wobbly water in times of need.

KIERAN HAYLER – for helping me burn off all of these calories and keeping me focused!

VICKS DICKSON – Thank you for stepping in at a time of need and really supporting me in my growth! A fellow Cancarian and lover of food…I adore you.

CLAIRE GREENAWAY - For being such a wonderful friend. I cannot wait to see what you're capable of with your own business! I am so proud of you.

DILLON, DELILAH, ROWLAND, MARYLIN, HARRY & PAMELA (MY CATS) – for shamelessly lying on my keyboard in the late hours. Nobody wants to eat ChILLLLLLLZEWESH or GARLIFFFFFFFFFFF. #Justsayin'.

…and finally…

MY BOYS. MY WORLD.

Thank you to Julian – your kindness and warmness knows no bounds. I am so proud of the little person that you are.

To Louis, my second born. You are amazing. Thank you for being such a charming and beautiful little chap.

I love you both more than anything. Always have and always will.

I love you all and I am more grateful than you will ever know.

Thank you.

Pollyanna
X